Noise and Whispers

GIRISH MEHTA

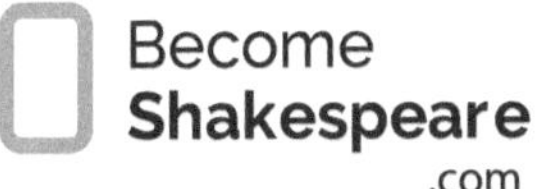
Become
Shakespeare
.com

First published in 2022 by
BecomeShakespeare.com

One Point Six Technologies Pvt Ltd.
119-123, 1st Floor, Building J2, B - Wing, WadalaTruck Terminal,
Wadala East, Mumbai, Maharashtra, India, 400022.
T:+91 8080226699

DISCLAIMER

This is a work of fiction. Unless otherwise indicated, all the names, characters, businesses, places, events and incidents except one in this book are either the product of the author's imagination or used in a fictitious manner. The resemblance to any actual person, living or dead, or actual events is purely coincidental.
The only known non-fictional name which has been used here is that of the Kapalkundala Kali Temple. In reality it is a very well preserved tourist spot in West Bengal. For the sake of the story it has been described as an abandoned and ill preserved place.

ISBN: 978-93-5559-159-3

Dedicated to Ruchira, my wife and rebel-in-house.

To my naughty and creative daughter, Zeisha!

And, to my parents, in-laws, Arjun, Prakhar - my nephews - You all are awesome!

Prologue

Some words, Some phrases.

This is my book of poems. A book that carries heartfelt poetry and thoughts penned during the various phases of my life.

In this book, I have written poems that take account of various emotions and feelings we humans experience.

I have also written about events we come across everyday that affect our hearts and minds. The poems are complimented with words I feel are important for me to say, to drive you to the aptness and feelings about these poems, the way they should be felt!

As a poet and writer, I look forward to making a connection with you and to take you on a rhythmic journey of words and prose. Well, sometimes non-rhyming too! Because, I believe expression should not be bound and should be free from the shackles of order, template and what has followed through generations.

Welcome to the emotions in the rain forest of my mind.

About the Author

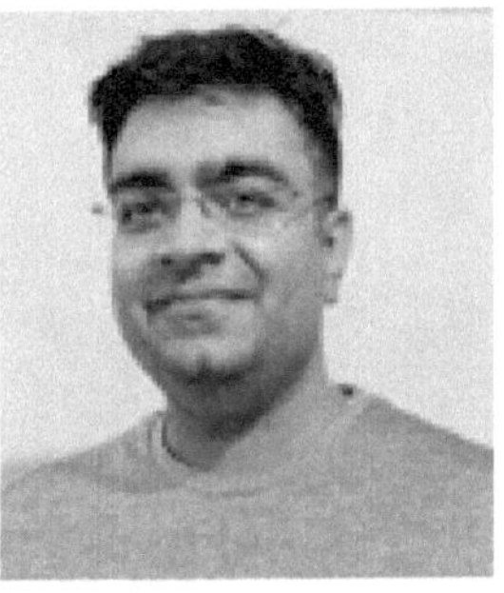

Girish Mehta is a Poet, Writer, and Entrepreneur who loves to write words and create ideas. He is based out of India and is a rebellious creative individual.

Contents

Birth – Evolution   9
Poem1   Raindrops, Puddles and Giggles   10
Poem 2 The Wait for Her   12
Poem 3 Bringing up Her   14
Hospitals, hope, and hope   17
Poem 4 - Defeating the fairies   18
The World that appears different   21
Poem 5 Botox   22
Poem 6 Storms inside the Past-boxes   24
Connecting with the Unknown   27
Poem 7 Psychedelic Chants   28
Breakups and Being Alone   31
Poem 8 Social Stigma   32
Poem 9 Wan't you why don't you want another friend   34
Nature and Vultures   37
Poem 10 The Pines Have Died   38
Poem 11 The Cold Hour and the Cuppa of Coffee   40
Poem 12 Hard to Find   42
War   45
Poem 13 The Battleschool of Iraq   46
Love   49
Poem 14 One thing is sure, love is not pure   50
Poem 15 Spaces   52
Poem 16 Jimmy wants you back   54
Poem 17 Happy Tom   56
Poem 18 Desperate for Love   58
Poem 19 Dare to leave me   60
Poem 20 Where I left a tone   62
Poem 21 The Wait Is Over   64

Inner Conflict   67

Poem 22 Yes I am alright   68

Poem 23 Playful Jiberesh   70

Poem 24 Purple affection   72

Poem 25 Some words, lots of words   74

Poem 26 To live   76

Poem 27 The love had begun   78

Poem 28 The Rules of the game   80

Poem 29 Change of Guard   82

Poem 30 Anxious Breaths   84

The Future - Children   87

Poem 31 The Child with a Dry Smile   88

Poem 32 The World in Her Eyes   90

Poem 33 The Still Pool Water   91

Poem 34 Arrogant Ocean Blue   92

Poem 35 Thankless Us   94

Poem 36 Lessons Can't be Learnt   96

Poem 37 Before You Go   98

Poem 38 Concentric Circles - Dream Inside a Dream   100

Poem 39 An Empty Paper, Sketches Itself   102

Birth – Evolution

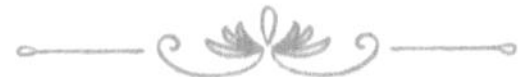

The truth on which this universe stands is the ability of living beings to reproduce. This leads to birth. In humans, it is a simple yet complicated phenomenon. But, it leads to emotions, some very deeply felt, some felt in passing.

Here are some words about a child who brought hope, comfort and satisfaction after a long and tiring battle in the thing called life. This entire world is populated by the human species and other distinct animals and birds. We experience birth everyday, yet we do not take a moment and pause at this wonder which keeps the universe functional and running.

Poem 1
Raindrops, Puddles and Giggles

When the raindrops come falling,

The kids giggle, mischief comes crawling.

The hurried mothers scurry for rain coats and high boots,

While kids try to peep through the windows hearing kids' hoots.

Puddles become jumping trampolins,

Raindrops become fairy friends.

With an innocent disregard,

My daughter wins her worlds in the rain showers withering.

There is a knocky knock,

She comes soaked in giggles.

Her mother warms the overnight soup,

With a feigned smile to keep fevers at bay.

She looks at her creation and smiles at heavens to always lead her way.

In rain and shine to always keep her in giggles and hay.

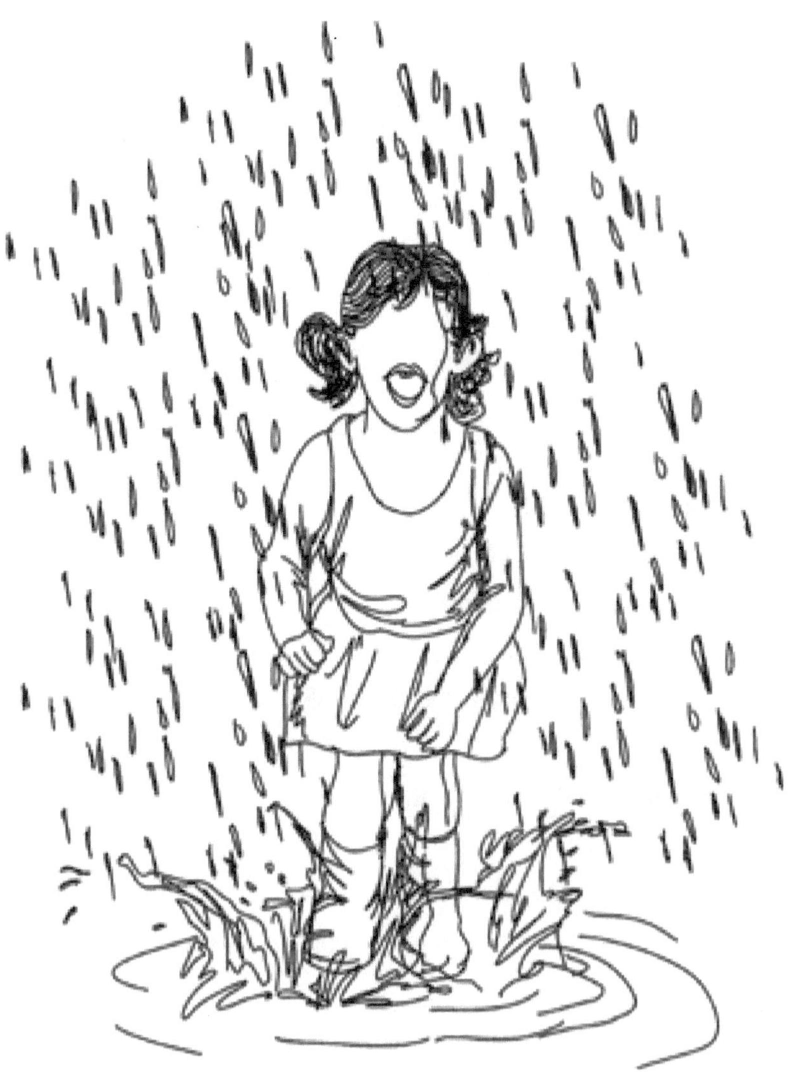

Poem 2
The Wait for Her

The doctor announced its on the way,

Always smile, don't be dismay.

Her wait was agonising,

The pain was real.

When I would feel nothing,

Her kicks would make it surreal.

I ate the blandest, stood on my toes,

The anxious moments all in my tow.

When she smiled and cried,

Her tears went through the waters that broke.

She cried and smiled into my worlds,

The wait was over.

But all this while? And her father's smile!

With his trust and love, he went to the moon and we walked a mile.

We waited for her,

And waited for her and waited for her.

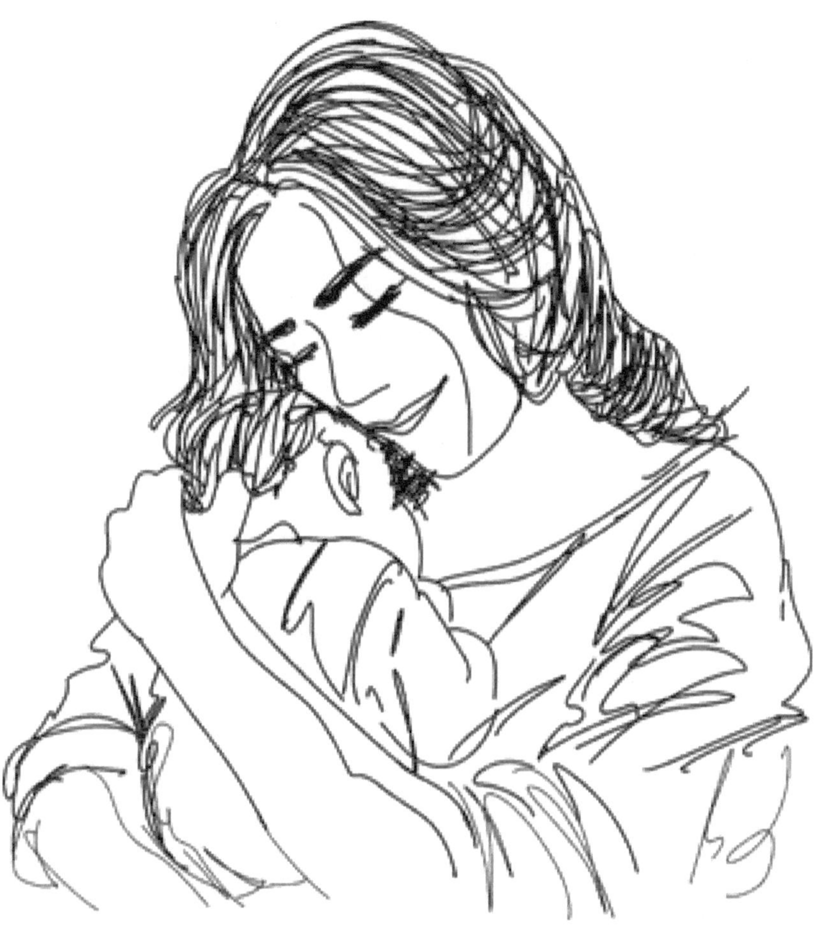

Poem 3
Bringing up Her

My stomach aches from the stiches they gave me,

Her welcome to the world was through the gates of my stomach.

I sleep when she wakes and wake up when she sleeps,

We lose track of the times and hours.

In a world that continues to hate,

We dance and chime,

To put a smile on her,

And feed her vegetables that grate.

A mother whose husband is soldiering in lands afar,

I bring her up, with love and life in ajar.

For when she grows up, she knows,

There were storms and winds, and she can brave them all.

She knows,

She is a woman who smiles and smiles and smiles.

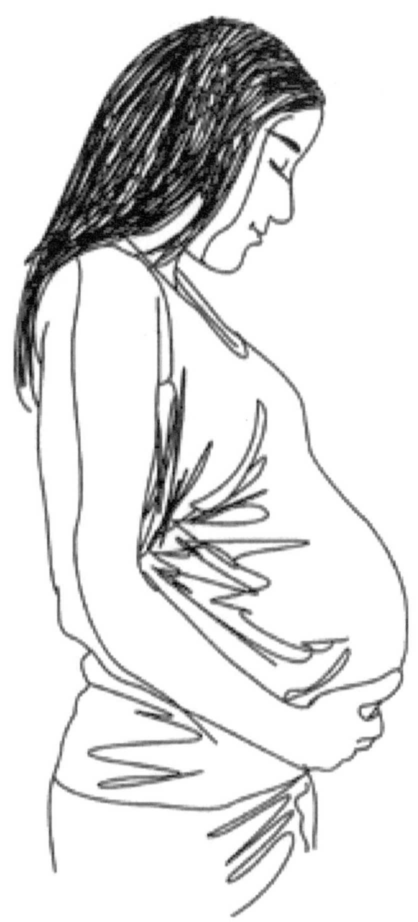

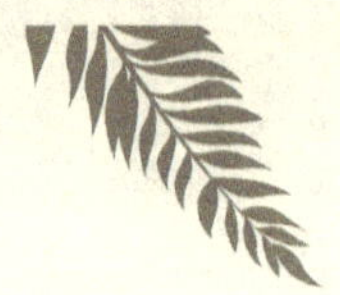

Hospitals, hope, and hope

A hospital is a circus of life and death. A poet observes this from a distance with a fear of lengthy bills and helplessness. Here are some words to empower fellow poets when they visit the sacred domes of medicine again. Hospitals are laden with stinky smells, greed, and no purity. But what if, you walk out of there with your hope intact.

The words that beat through your heart when they drag your loved ones through the corridors trying to save them, leave a special place in your heart. It could be a mother, a wife, a friend or even a stranger you meet in a medical institution, it makes you question the whole barter system of pain and gain.

Poem 4
Defeating the fairies

She lay on the table of test
her destiny in the hands of the surgeon

Fighting the syringes, drips and bottles of blood
I shed a tear fearing a flood

she lay she smiled bidding the final farewell
her smile captured in my heart in a thousand flashes

dad counting the pounds and pennies increasing by each drip
trying to be oblivious of the dark dungeons ahead

Her inner soul giving up and wanting to be smuggled to heaven
I the son only separated by the umbilical chord of nature

constantly praying to the man upstairs not to stamp her clearance papers
I kneeled down in front of hope, An atheist in prayer

Her son, only separated by the umbilical chord of nature
The red light extinguished and out came she came

alive, smiling - the diva the dame

I checked out of the medical resort

defeating the fairies once again till death do us apart

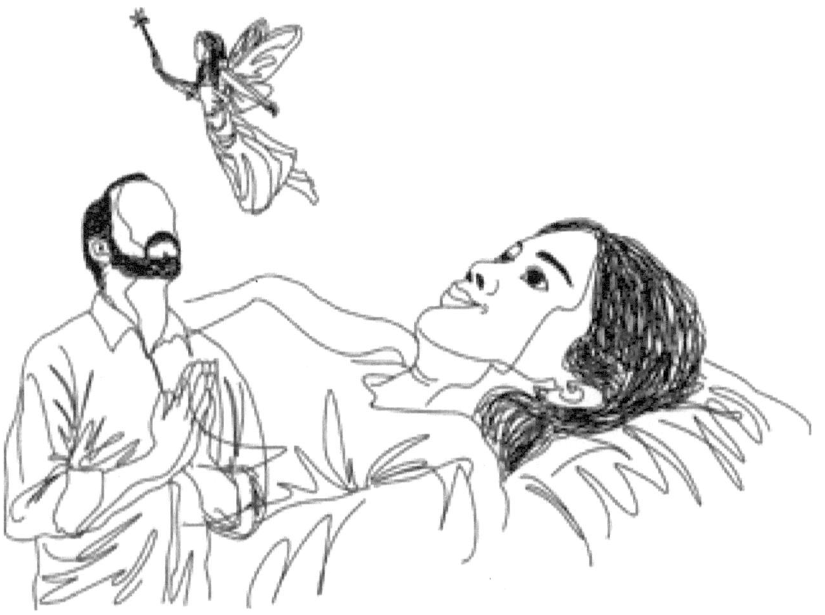

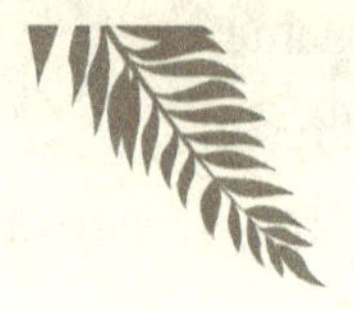

The World that appears different

We prepare and prepare for the world, for the questions that wait us outside the safe walls of our house. And yet, we put up a show, sing a hymn and do the dance of the world.

Here is to the wars between the inner you and the external world. Between the smiles you expect but the snobbishness you come across. The manipulations you receive and the regrets that go by.

Here is a poet helplessly looking at these emotions and also in control of these emotions with verse.

Poem 5
Botox

When I was in school,
Mum covered my blemishes with talcum powder.

When I went to college, dad botched my grades with a medical certificate
And taught me to fight honest, and be modest.

Love knocked, sped an arrow,
I stumbled, paid for it with my blood sputtered tears.

My shrink taught me to whistle,
I humbled into the monotony of life.

All through it, I smiled, I laughed,
I joked, and I clowned a laugh, staged a heroic mimic.

And now they fret smiling, 'cos after every smile
they worry getting a botox.

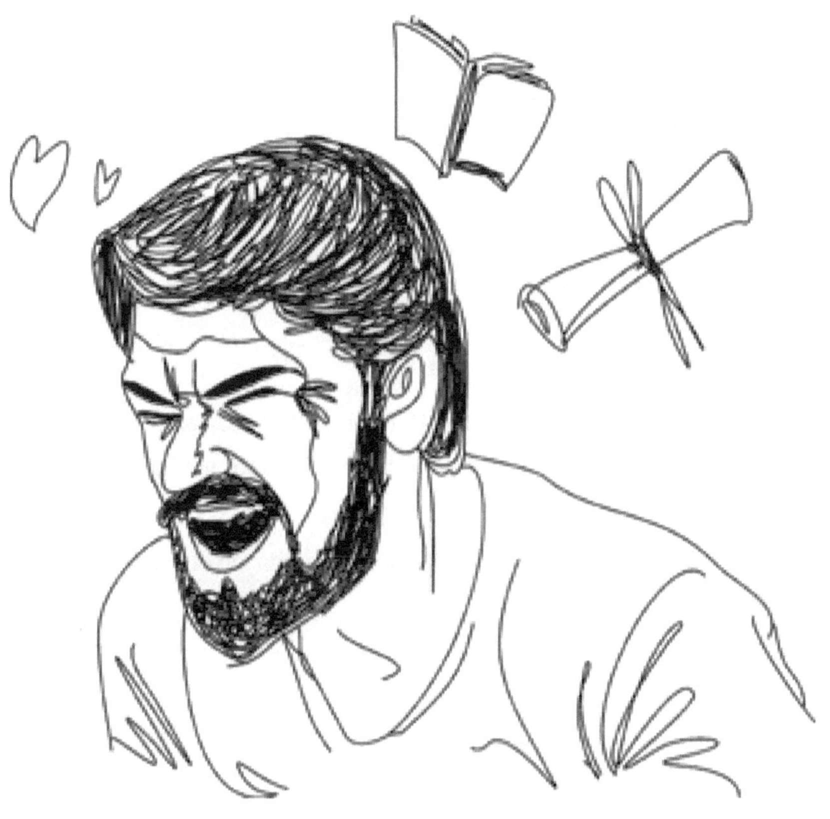

Poem 6
Storms inside the Past-boxes

I stood in the storm, whistling through the dust
They took offence and questioned my intent

The storm had passed; I dusted off the dust,
But they still wanted me to visit the cleaners.

Past was a perseverance elders were not ready to let go,
They were holding on to it like a mistress on instalment payments.

Success tip-toed like a careless silhouette towards me on an angry moon-night,
The shadow was kicked away by the ghosts of a stubborn past

Forced into the spiritual, I smiled at them
Wished them luck, and set out on my journey

I wish though, I had not crushed the thorns while picking up the flowers,
For thorns have a life of their own too!

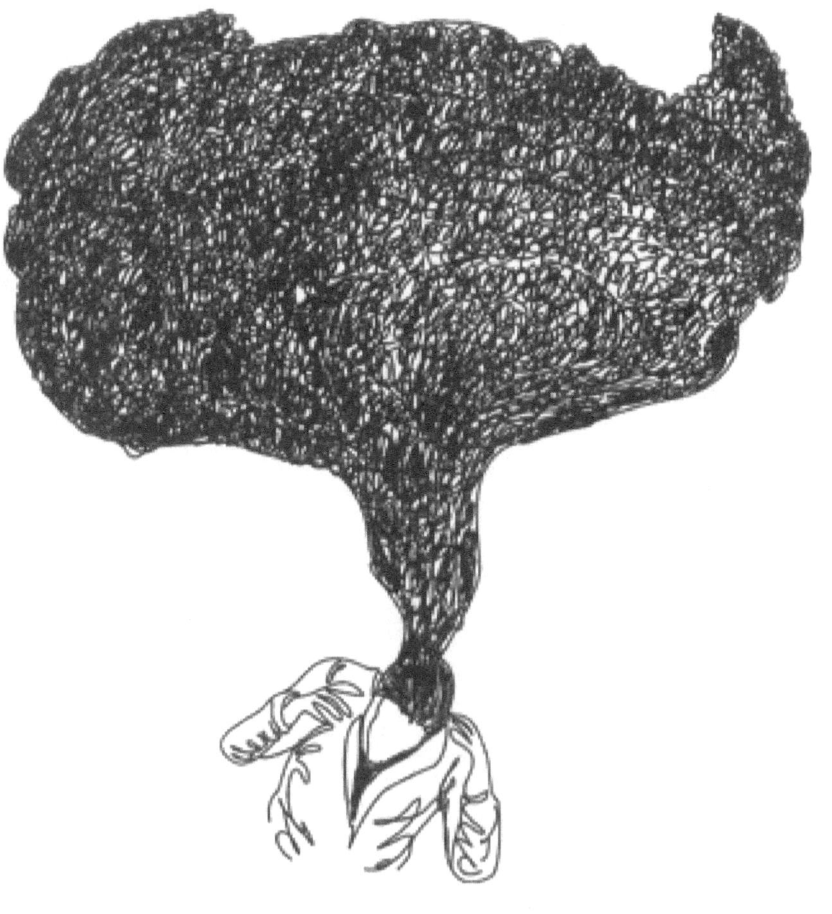

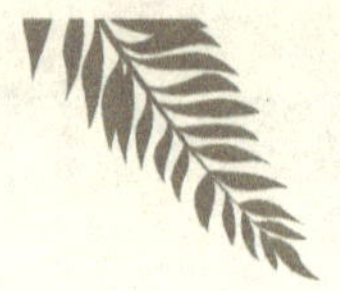

Connecting with the Unknown

Those voices in your head, those hunches that never leave you, the sky that you look at above – Hoping! That there is a world beyond us, where they watch us, giving us pain or easing it when we can't take it anymore.

Connecting with the psyche is an experience in its own. Some look at it in a positive way while some look down on it. In one way or another, it exists!

Poem 7
Psychedelic Chants

I stand in the temple of God,
Before I begin my crazy dance I look up to him for a Nod

Clamp Clonk, Clamp Clonk
The bangles hit and the drums honk

Anger and love for him inside me
I have lost I have wandered and he secretly hit me

Trampling on misery and faith, on a cold sweat of a bait
I smile and hate him for the vices and hate

The chants fill my psyche with happiness and hope
The Psychedelic chants are 80% cocaine and 20% dope

My being will sway to the chant, till I can dance on his tunes,
The day you give up on me,
The temple would be haunted and the snakes will feast on the prunes.

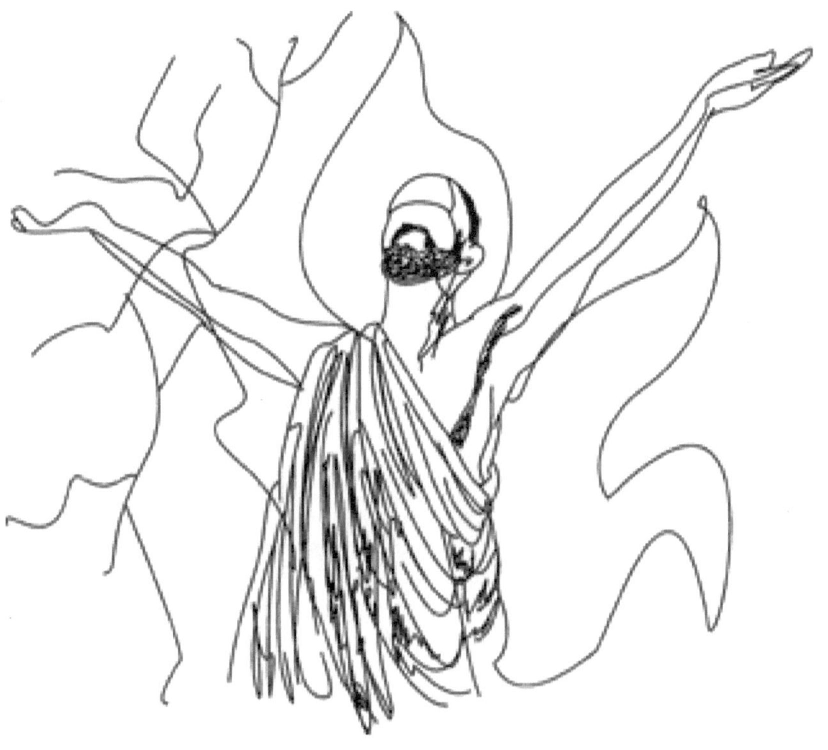

Breakups and Being Alone

They say, when you get hurt, when a heart breaks, no one can see or hear the pain, except you. While the world goes around in a merry go round, you question beliefs, people, and ask why me? And, more than that the stigma of divorce, breakups and the loneliness that ensues.

But what is stigma without overcoming things without poetry. A poet often rebels the world with words of their own.

Poem 8
Social Stigma

Some thought we digressed, some thought we lost touch

Some thought we went aloof, fighting the social battles all alone

Some waited for spring to arrive, some for letters from us

Some complained they missed the parties, the wine with the humus

We told them in vain, love wasn't around It was hard to explain, that we were going away, directions south-bound

It snapped, tore us apart the cranberries and the pecans seemed tasteless, so did the apple tart

The stigmatic pragmatic elders didn't help, The ruthless and the nosey on whom I wanted yelp

A ship may sink, ruins may float It's the stigma of a breakup which makes you bloat!

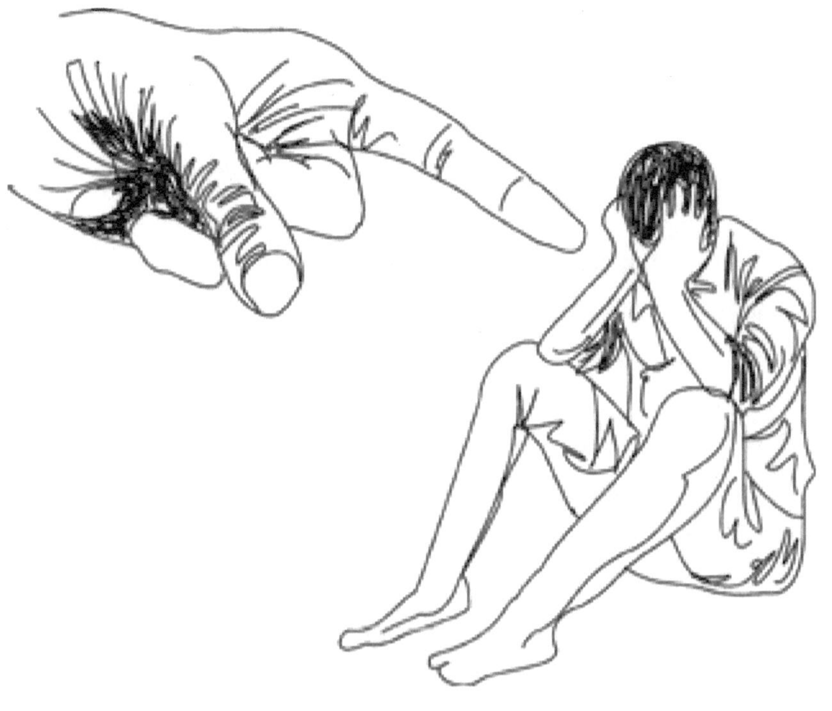

Poem 9
Wan't you why don't you want another friend

Someone to talk to, to hit you by the sheer power of love

Someone you can scold, talk, walk hand in hand with your glove.

Someone who can bring you out of the comma of sadness

Strange, isn't it, you'll still not befriend a stranger's madness

I know it's tough being part of a stranger's madness.

Because you never had it so good a friend for free in your loneliness

In your dreams you have thought of a friend who behaves exactly as you like,

Who sings, dances, plays and behaves as you like.

So don't worry I am not really coming in your life.

But I will give a hope that one day I'll come in your life

As a hope as a friend, You will wait in for me, I will walk into your life.

I will make you happy, that day will come.

Would be sad for some and happy for some.

I am saying this with a hole in my heart.

Cos I am also still looking for that selfless hearty friend.

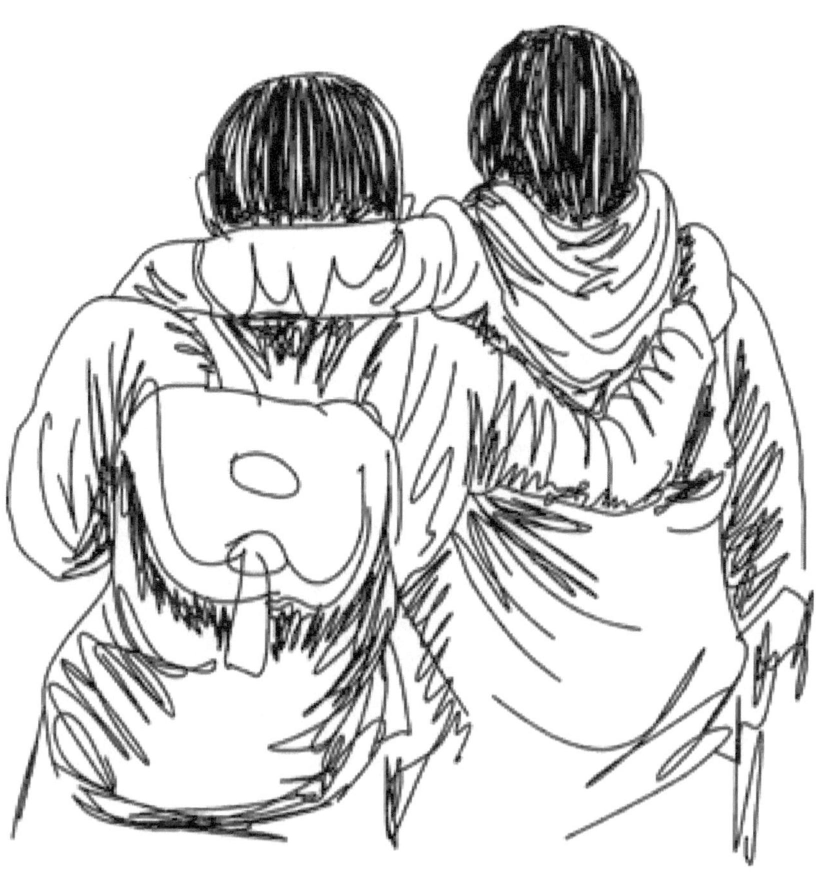

Nature and Vultures

People blame vultures for being mean and flesh eaters while we happily feast at the limited resources mother earth has. We put out fires patting ourselves at our own back for fires we only created, for killing dolphins that will never smile again, for eliminating forests that will never give us air to breathe, again.

There is not an inch of earth spared by humans, where will we go once there is no earth left.

Poem 10
The Pines Have Died

There used to be beautiful pines in the countryside of Alabama

They looked very divine to my mama.

The pines were used for decoration

Some even used them for spiritual salvation.

The children used to play along

They used to sing Alalalalala pine song

They were the talk of the town

Beautiful like a broach on mother earth's gown.

But they were set on fire.

And thus, was gone everybody's desire

They couldn't take the hatred of today

Everybody wanted to kill them cut them sell them and make hay

The gentleness of the pine was transformed into anger

Now they wanted to don he robe of the avenger

So they the humble the cute they killed themselves

They embraced the hot burning fires into their selves

Now I am searching for them where they have gone

Look! Says a small child the pines have died down.

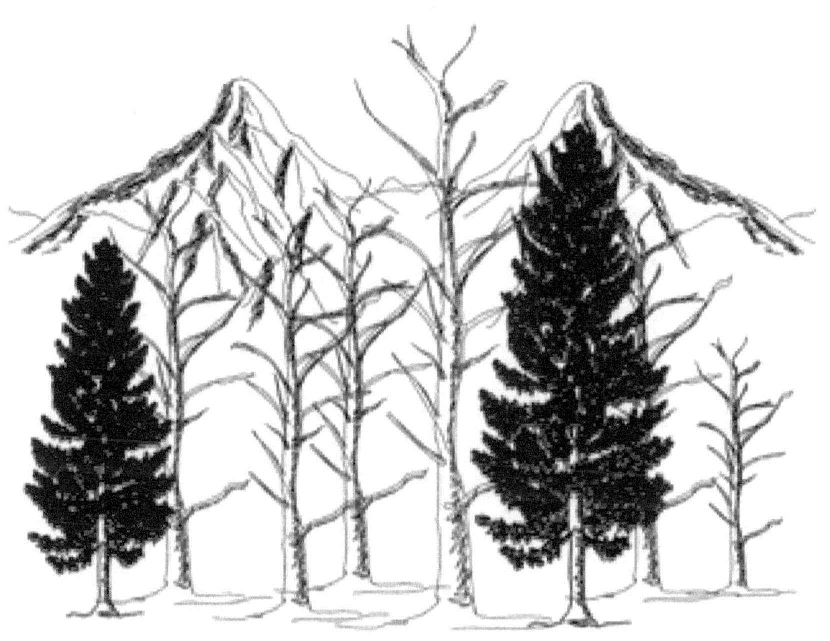

Poem 11
The Cold Hour and the Cuppa of Coffee

There is coldness in the air. We sip the coffee beans from the African workers.

The milk is synthetic and sugar made artificially in a farm far far away.

It's a cold hour, the world is crumbling with blasts and pasts. Wars being fought in all corners.

Skies are red, water's have lost their hue,

People are running amok, old wars turning new.

I sip my coffee, worried, in a thought which is old, not new.

The cold hours run by in the world, before the clock turns blue.

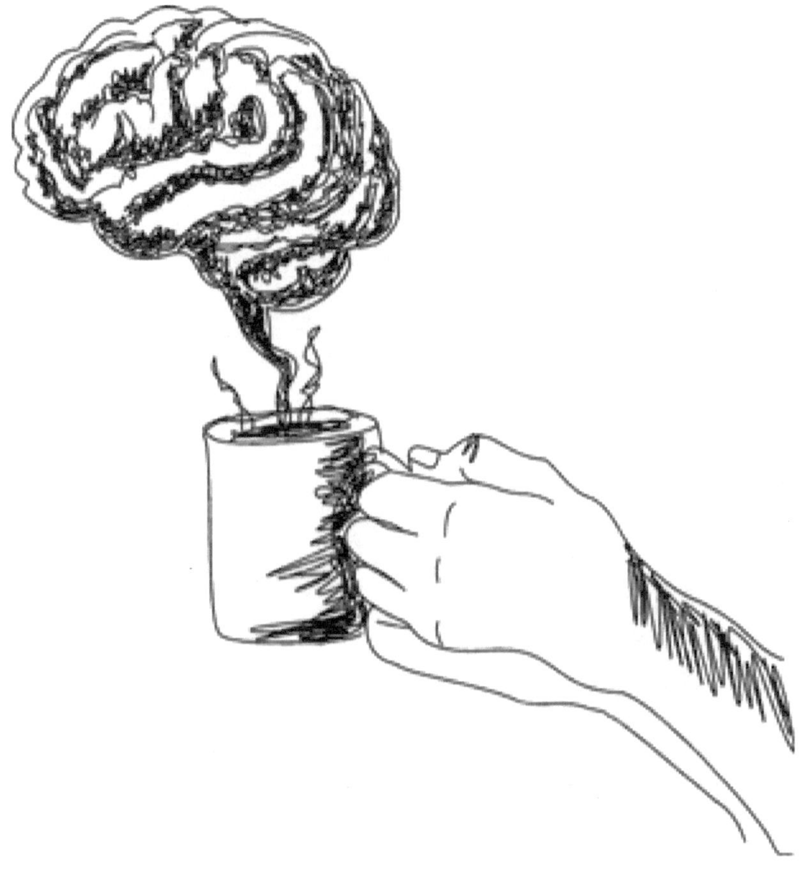

Poem 12
Hard to Find

Welcome to the world of sin and paradise,

Nobody even remembers anybody's demise.

Wherever you go, wherever you rise,

You see ash you see surprise.

Love, affection, respect, attraction

These are history, these are distractions.

But wise people tell me,

My elder ones yell me.

There would be light,

With all its might

The round cute orange,

Sun would shine bright

So hold on people, you are gonna have a wonderful bumpy ride,

You will call this world your home with pride.

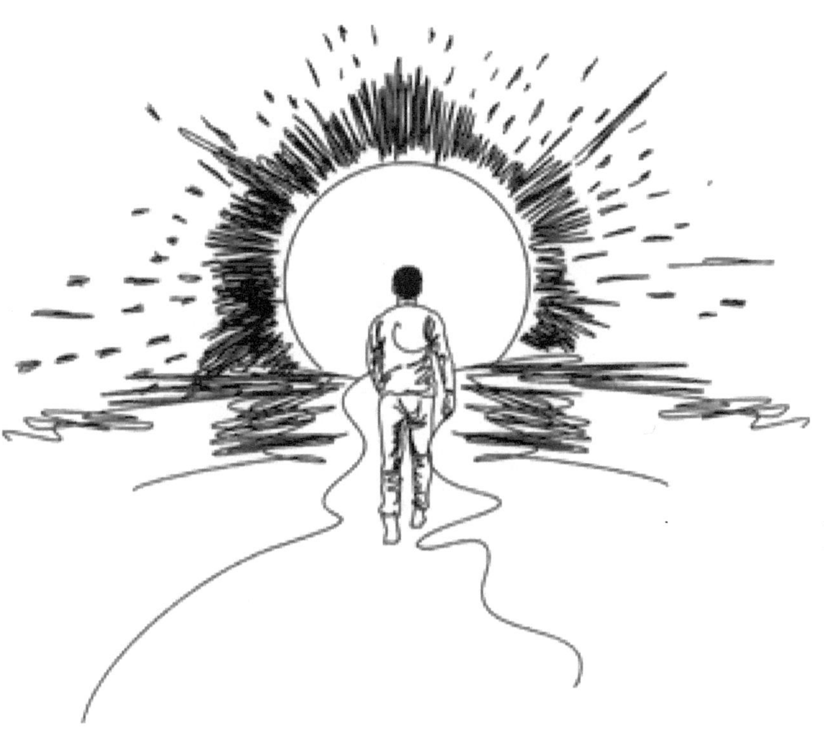

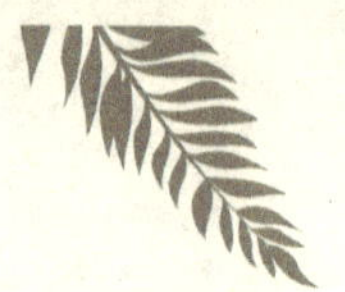

War

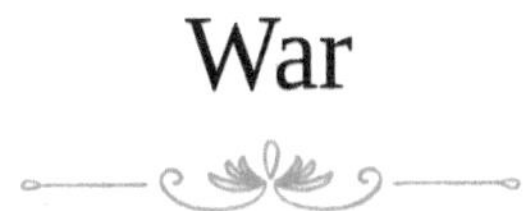

Battling over trivial stretches of land, shredding innocent bodies and children into pieces. War lends a failing sense of power to those who yearn for heads to bow.

But, millions lose a home, a peace they have yearned for and their ability to believe this birth is a gift to smile. Here we take a look at war and what it does to us.

Poem 13
The Battleschool of Iraq

Please tell bush please tell saddam

This war thing would kill adam

Already there are problems there is hate

Everybody's having problems with their mate

Please tell bush please tell saddam,

This War thing would kill the beautiful madame

This mother lover sister friend madame

Guns don't kill nor do bombs

Its people who kill each other and destroy the wombs

Please tell bush please tell saddam

Nothing would be left not even a palm

We all die one day

And with us wouldn't even take a qualm

There are already problems of life caste religion hate

Already is sorry the state of our fate

Please tell bush please tell Saddam

War would hurt bush and would Saddam

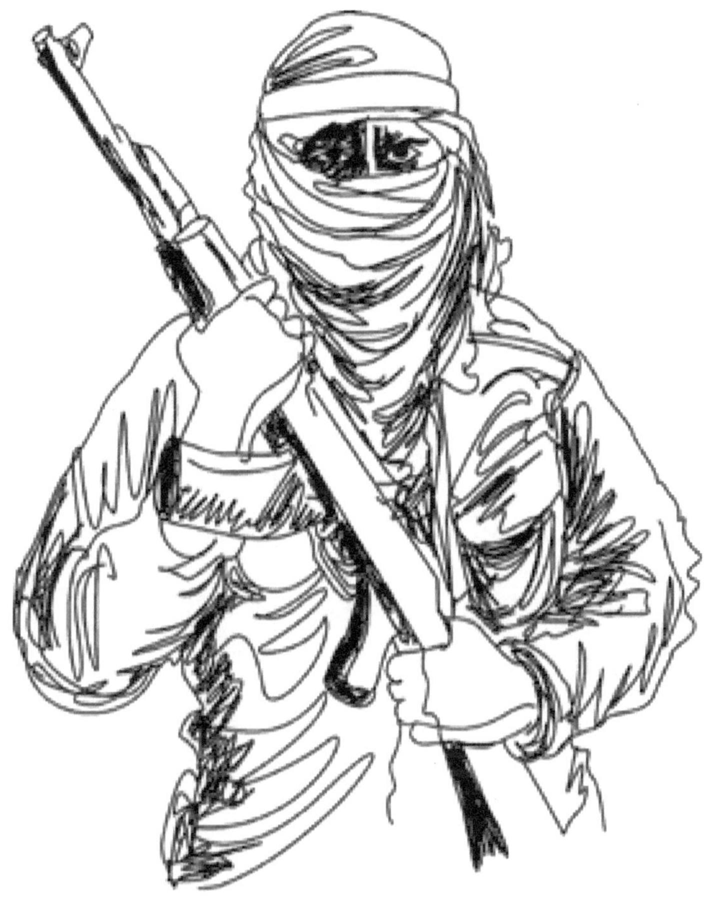

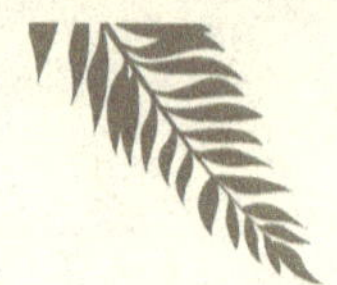

Love

The most written about, talked about emotion. The feeling that sends shivers in your stomach, the smile no one can wipe away or the constant yearning for that someone you are never going to meet again.

We have yearned for ages for true love and to find the true meaning of love, but what if there is no meaning to it. Only poetry.

Poem 14
One thing is sure, love is not pure

There is a heart burn, call missing friends, call missing love

Never had I had so tight

Life is looking like a rough black desert

People laugh on me, think I am funny

I am absurd,

I am ill, I need a pill,

Now who turn off the lights

They smile at me

This world provides dental physical motor insurance

But do they provide emotional insurance

Do they sell it anywhere, I am ready to pay for it

I am ready to sell myself to buy love.

To purchase emotions to see if there is a guarantee

One thing is sure, love is not pure.

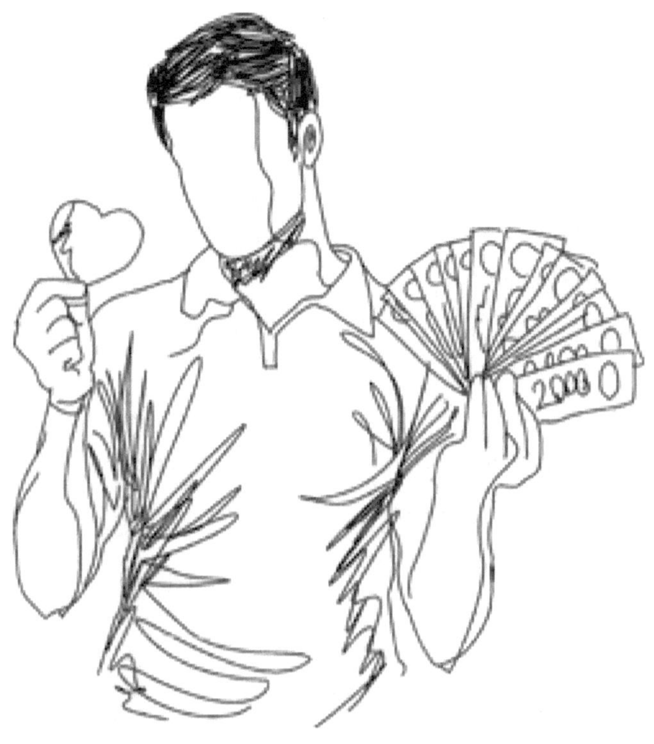

2000

Poem 15
Spaces

I drive through roads, unchallenged by their emptiness

Skipping signals, crushing a rabbit here and there.

I squat around in empty buildings,

Ordering take out and hearing loud echoes.

Avoid the mirrors but love conversations, with my beautiful mind.

Like a genius caged in a city with no humans, only people worrying about their next meal.

The garden with daughters, the bar with careless teens,

The markets with healthy women buying big vegetables.

Some easy places are still attractive to me.

The bazaars with a sudden burst of colors.

An occasional smile from a single mom with a truckload of emotions, and a cart of devotions.

Some spaces the society defined for me,

Like hospitals with expensive deaths.

Clothes hanging with silk threads, a space expensive somewhere to

Share an agent of completion.

A space not my own but paid in dues to them,

A space you own but, call it mine, to charge an expensive line.

Spaces everywhere, yet no space for me to breathe in time.

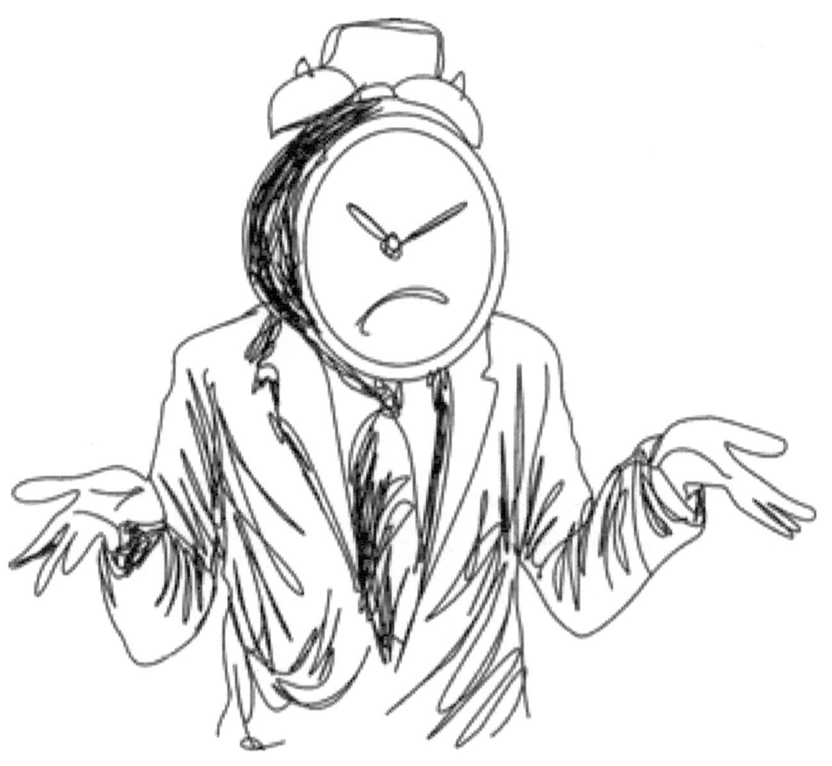

Poem 16
Jimmy wants you back

I wish words were moist,

I would send them on a dew to you.

I wish promises could be smelled,

I would have crushed them on a rose.

There was so much that could have gone right,

Jimmy tried hard with a heavy might.

Frogs, roses, champagnes,

It would have been an adventure.

You left jimmy in a dying flask,

Like clasping a live mommy in a coffin.

Jimmy wants you back,

Wherever you are here, drop him a smile.

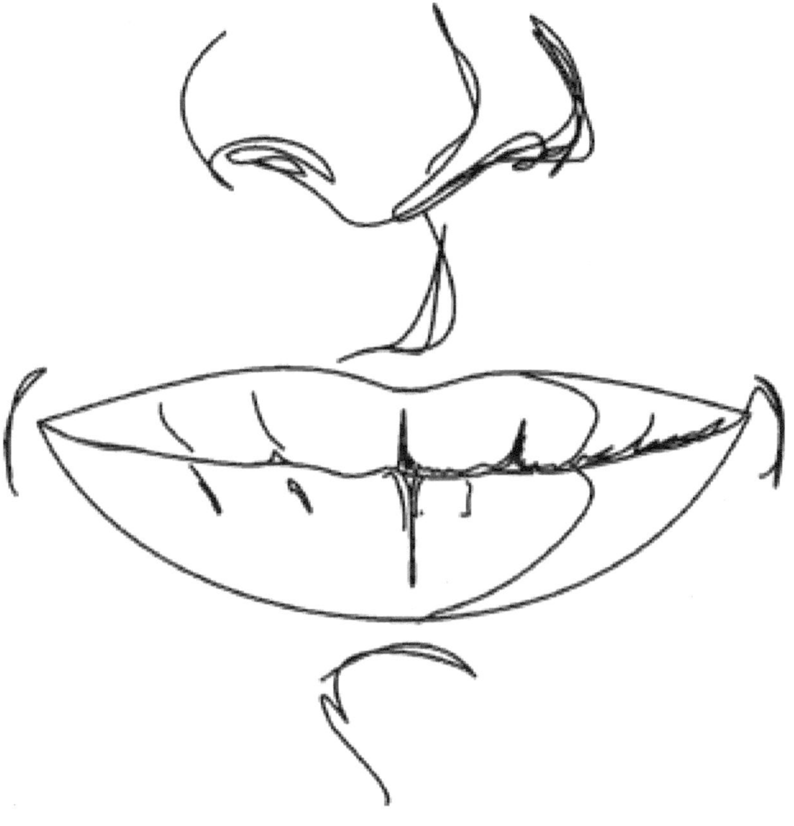

Poem 17
Happy Tom

Bouncy, funny, like a glutton.

Munching on a sweet loaf of mutton.

Happy Tom was a clown,

The laughing stock of northern brown

Missed in all the sad happenings,

His one liners start the gigglings.

He was a loved one,

Amongst the hated tonnes.

Sad tom was loved by someone,

The heart broke and he stuck a fake smile to his face.

Now everyone loves the happy tom.

And the happy tom misses the sad tom.

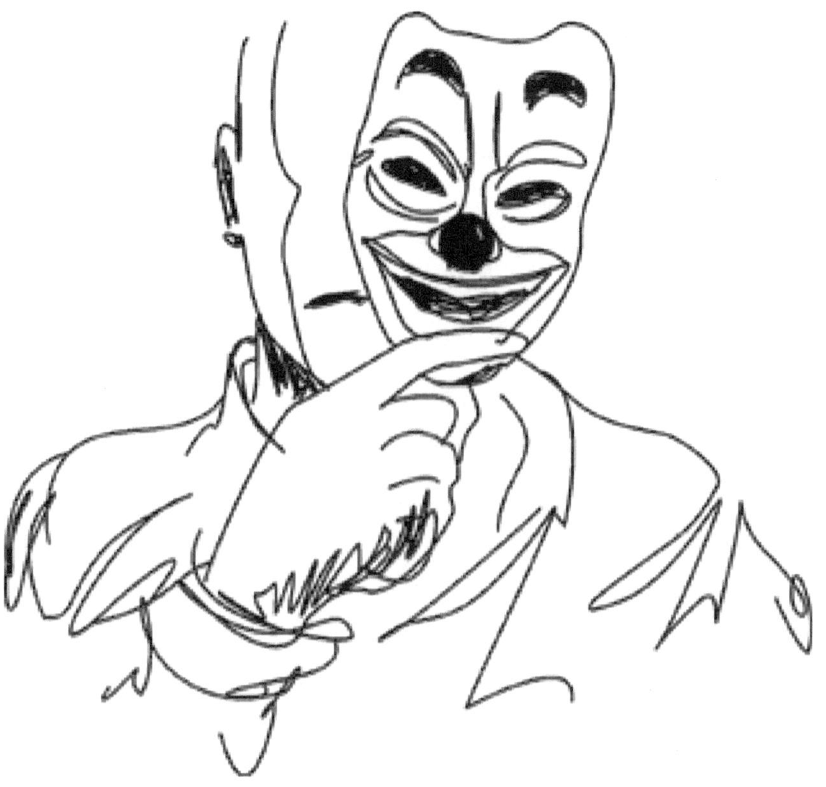

Poem 18
Desperate for Love

Air flows through me but I cant breathe,

I want to lie but can't succeed.

I've seen girls and guys,

Being gifted expensive toys.

Want to be with them,

Want to live with them.

The problem is I'm looking for affection,

To end my gruesome lonely exilation.

Already been to morocco, been to Japan,

Roamed in beijing and in Sudan.

I've strayed aimlessly in the streets,

Seen other people enjoying their treats.

I don't ask for money, not for fame.

All I want is one pretty dame.

I'm not in the rat race to marry,

After seeing what happened to poor harry.

She left him cold, alone to die,

He eventually took poison in an apple pie.

But still I want to be bitten, not to be spared – carelessly smitten.

For love is a sacrifice, not a luxury.

I want to be in love for I'm in a great hurry.

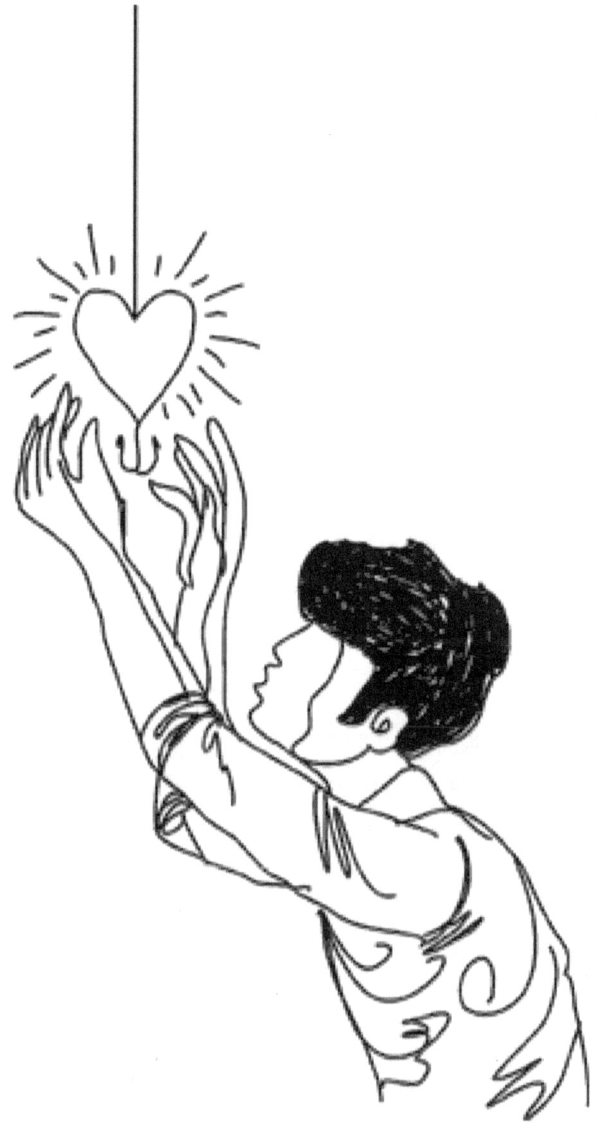

Poem 19
Dare to leave me

I want you for the days you promised I would be happy

For the empty straws, crushed napkins and giggles we left in cafes.

There were seasons, and suns, and raindrops.

And we used to be happy.

Then we parted ways, and you wanted to smile more

But looked more sad at it, than happy.

I waited near the lamp post where we sang, we knitted a dream

It was a wait worthwhile, I collected a sheen.

Where are we with the promises that never came,

We never saw the happy walks embodied in a frame.

You dare to leave me and walk away into an oblivion,

I will walk the fields like a Sufi, with my head sprinkled with vermillion.

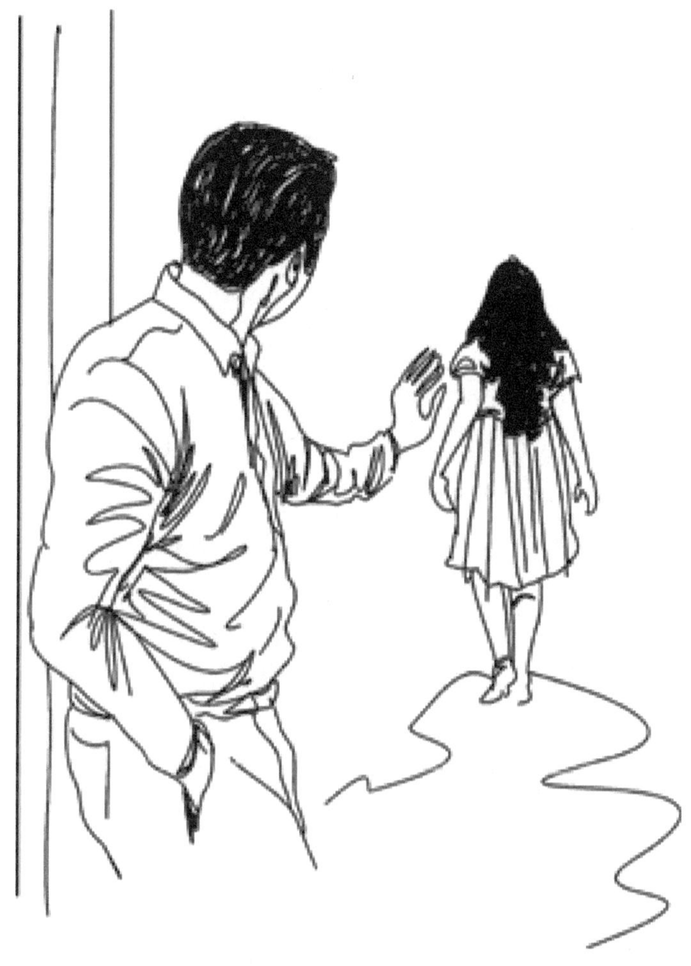

Poem 20
Where I left a tone

So I'll start from where I left

I was a happy soul, never alone

Singing the happy tone.

Before that I used to be dejected.

Always everywhere, always rejected.

Now, I am back to the business I am more happy when I am sad,

The clouds have again turned black.

I picked up the notes, where G Minor would fit in a tone,

I strum and string, to a monotone.

They will remember my words, when I am alone,

When they are alone, when there would be no tone.

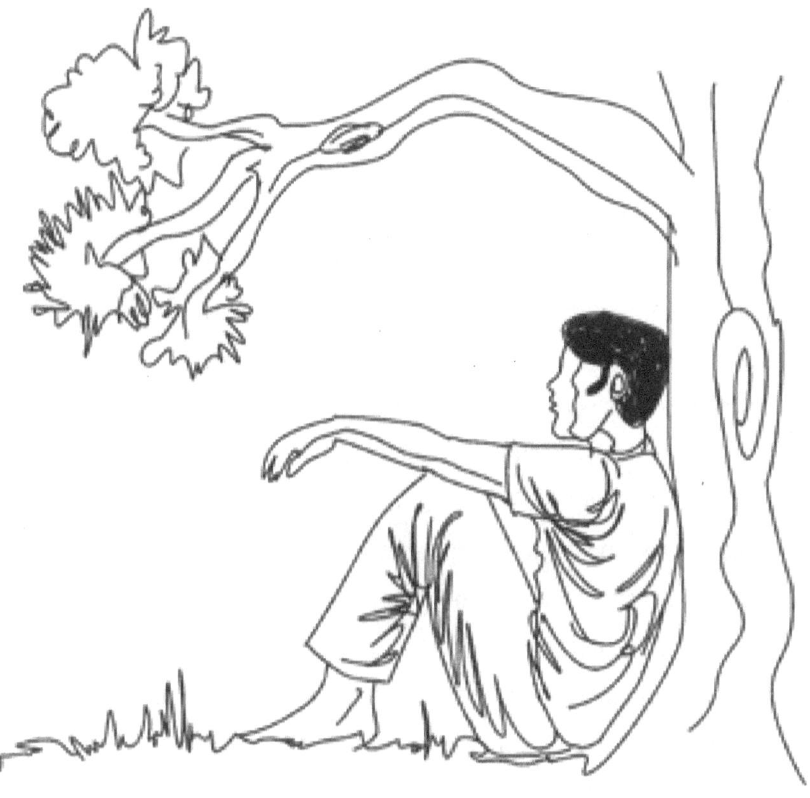

Poem 21
The Wait Is Over

The wait is over

Says the poetic Mr. Rover

Now you don't have to wait for trouble in queue

It is always coming to you as if it was long due

The silent days are over, no use longing for the landrover

Its sadness and madness everywhere and all over

Even the poets, the carefree, lovable, nice poets are having a tough time

They are starving, bankrupt without a dime

The state of the heart is also not great.

It pains all the time, sinks all the time, as if it was too late mate.

The doctor says take a medicine, you have stress.

But how do I tell him I can't pay him, I am already in distress

Whatever happened to the lord of life who used to give happiness,

Who used to shower love and finish our loneliness.

The wait is over, the Skys have spoken,

No one is holding your flag, its you and you only, riding into the sunsets.

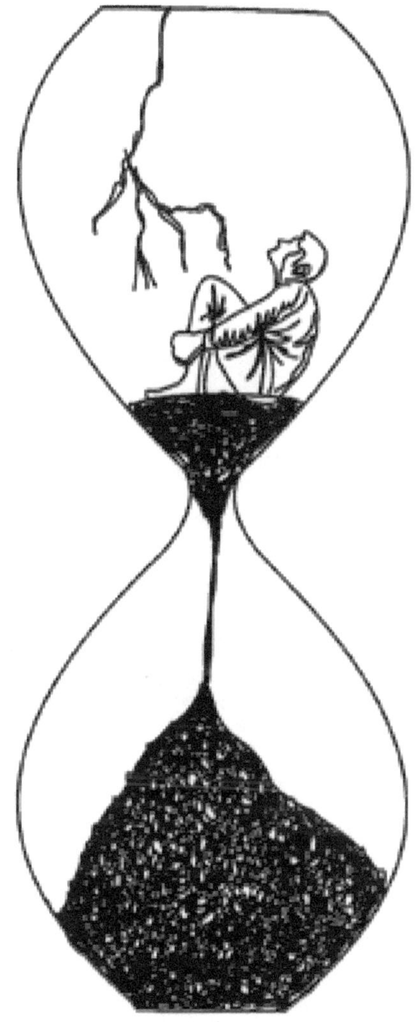

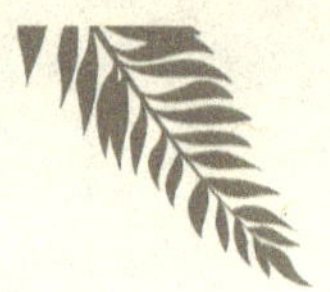

Inner Conflict

When there is conflict inside you. Everything seems right and wrong at the same time. It's an interesting mix of verse and words then. Anxiety and practical decisions have a long conversation at your sleep's expense.

So, we put a smile, after a while and let the conflicts tussle. While we get on with our everyday lives, earn a bread and grow older.

Poem 22
Yes I am alright

This world tried to break me with all its might,

But I was holding very tight.

The sun always shone very bright,

A young girl walked past me holding light,

Cherichikchchcickin chu alright.

Kwak attack hold on could'nt have been worse alright.

The unmistakable rhythm of poetry,

As if the perfect aroma of an eatery.

The mixed effect of the fixed lines,

The fixed effect of the mixed lines.

The singular effect of the plurals,

I'm sounding someone from the rurals.

I'm timid as a rat, solid as a Rambo.

But whenever I'm happy I like to do the Tango.

Like eating a mango.

Boy this rhythm thing is getting over me.

Poetry is like a fever, please get away from me.

But so heavenly is the effect of it please don't leave me.

I like to cry I like to whine I like to cry.

I like to live I like to love I like to flirt I like to fly.

I will slow down on the rhythm fever, cos I'm not alone in the mad rush
I have you to walk with me.

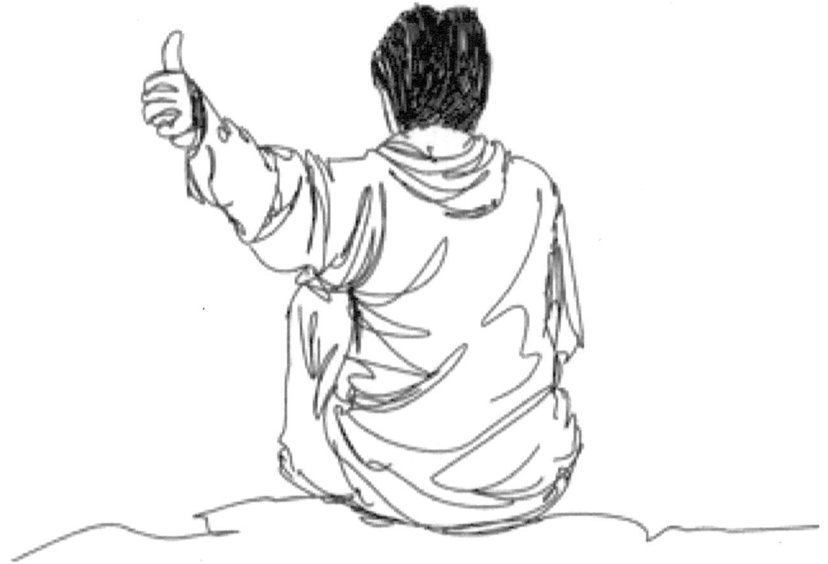

Poem 23
Playful Jiberesh

I sat on a burning flying bear.

Rode till the start of death,

Flew to kansas on a Friday,

Irrespective of my deed.

I summed up a cyclone,

Playful hurting crying heart.

There is a certain order in confusion,

When you write and spring up word after word.

And leave poetry and rhythm far behind,

In the world of feelings, order and mayhem.

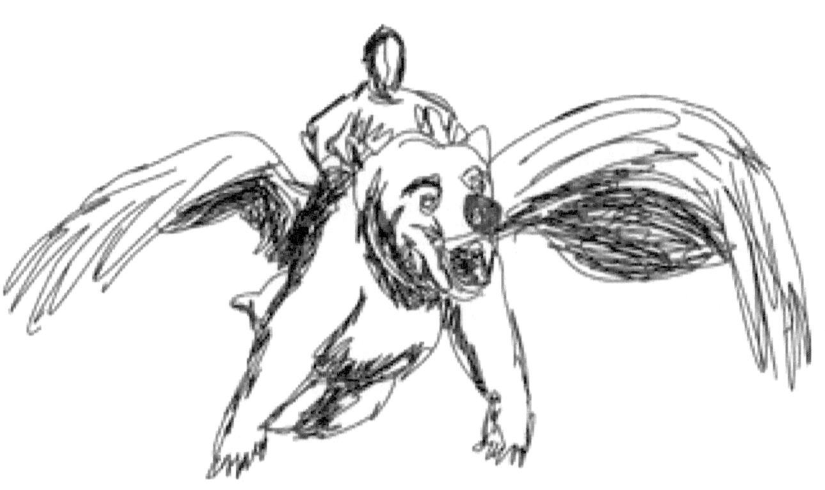

Poem 24
Purple affection

Inscrutable vanity purple affection

Die on the banks

River number one

Whisper in my ears

Thou Warmth I seek

I'll weep if you don't, I'll drop if you whine

Nothing compares to your love

Your touch Your grin

Aah! And your cold skin

I run for love

I try to sing

Hot blood in me

I still rule your heart

Though you hate me

I'm..I'm lonely without you.

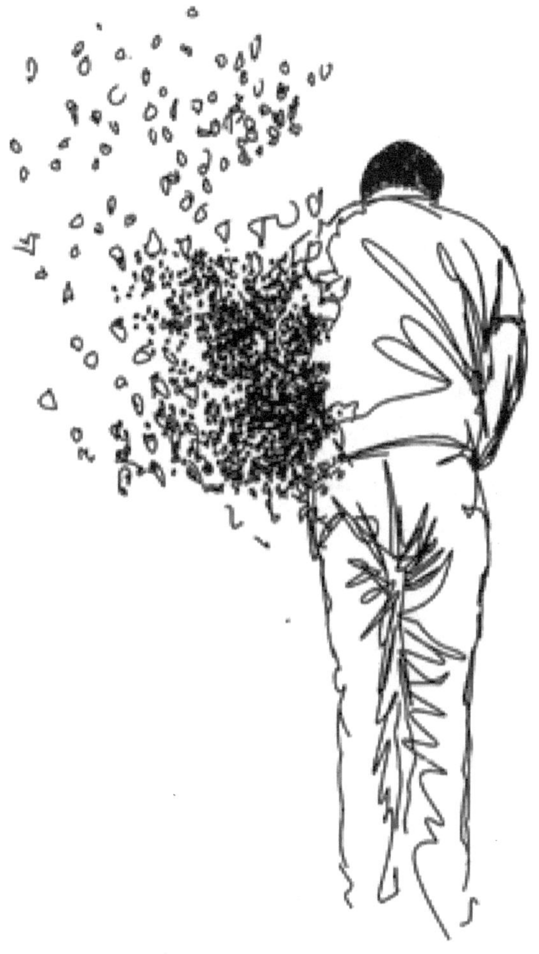

Poem 25
Some words, lots of words

Tresspasser Prosectuted, Health

Earring reading Ewan fiction hard.

Pirate boom, Catapault lips love.

Harsh alone, tea walk, fat airs.

Headalong, stop marriage, bus mother.

Breakfast beautiful forgive ask,

Request return mobile ring tones.

Mumble rob steal walkman ticket,

Walk eat patty-ies stare, ogle.

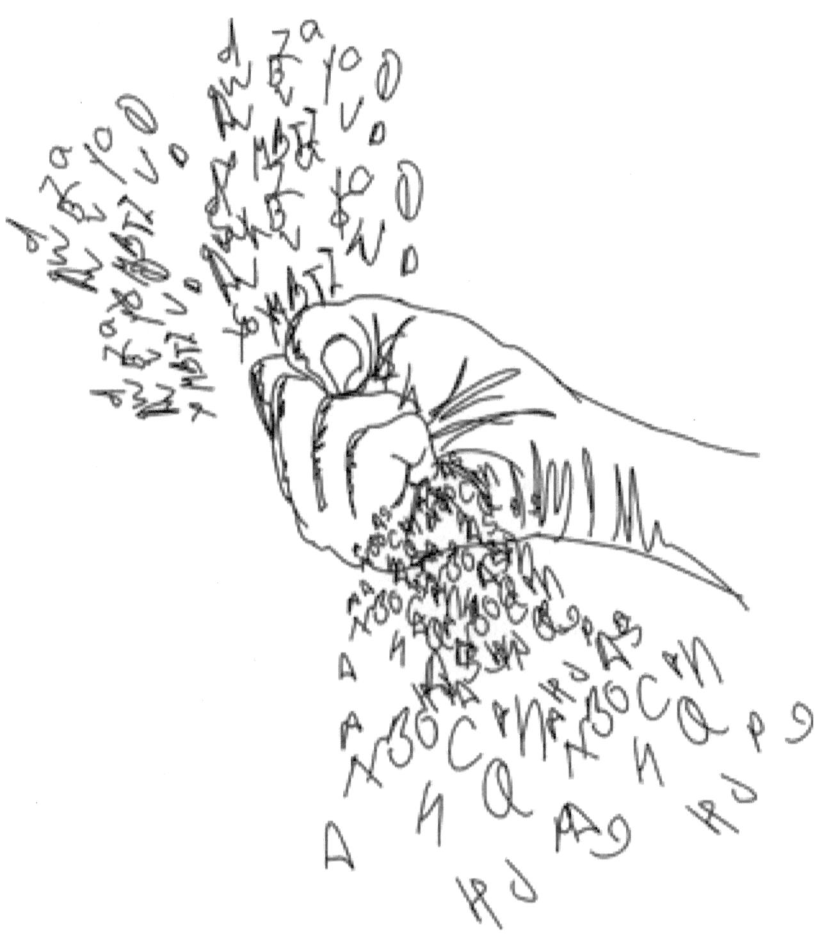

Poem 26
To live

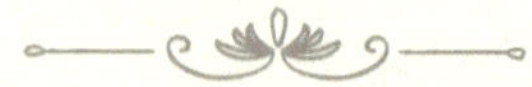

To live to die

We love we lie

Post to pillar

Like a clown, like a caterpillar

We earn, we yearn,

Somewhere we burn.

We fight wars, save the bombs,

Burn the tombs, then build the armies.

We save money, to die an untimely death,

We live, we thrive, sometimes we are naive.

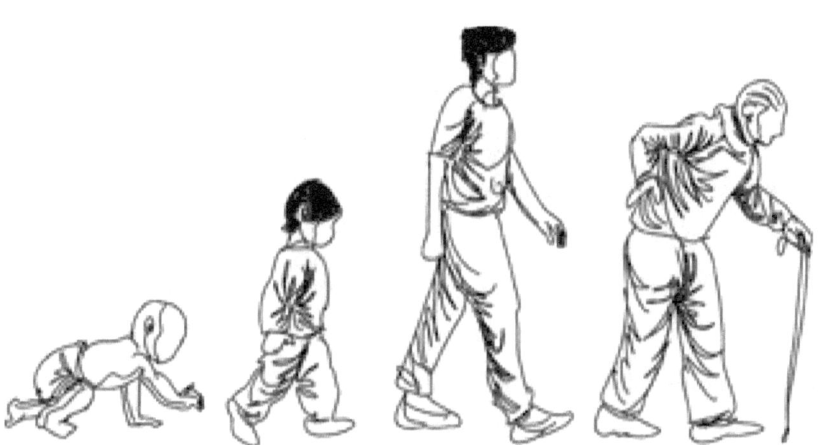

Poem 27
The love had begun

The blunder had already been done,

A love story in making had already begun

I watched in blunder, the clouds had a thunder.

At the crossroads, she smiled a careless smile.

The love had begun,

The forests were gonna burn.

We stood opposed.

She fairer and richer than me,

I, the Road Romeo waiting in the wings.

The families hated each other,

The Mothers sniped one another.

We wanted to hold hands more,

The love begun, blossomed and lived forever in the cemetery of our minds.

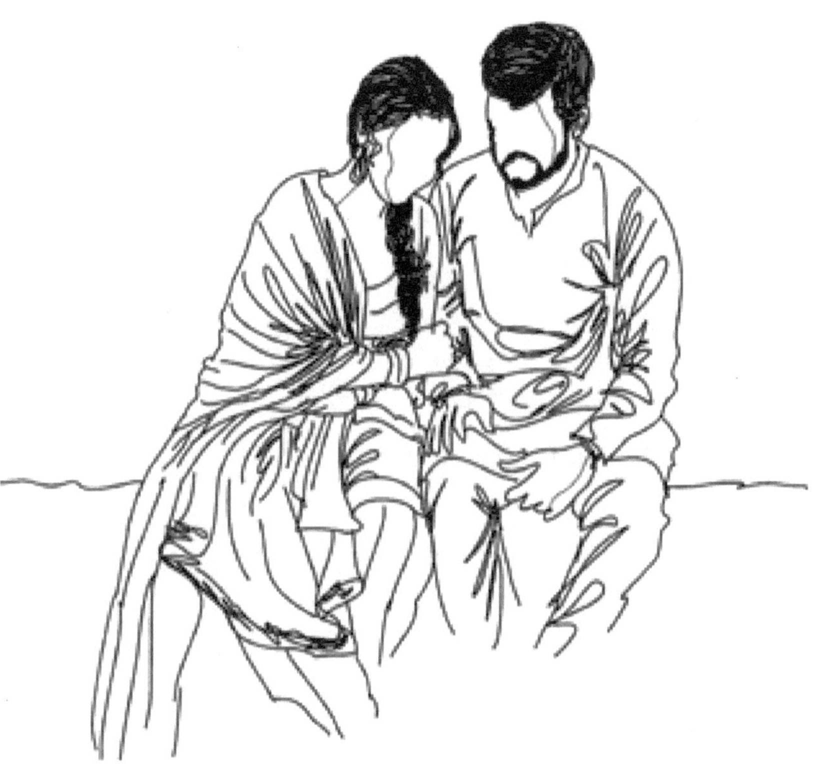

Poem 28
The Rules of the game

How to win a woman

I'm not a flirt nor a hearththrob nor a hunk

Sometimes I am looking like a punk.

I m no brad nor a ricky

I am ugly, nice and funny like mickey

But I know the rules of the game

Whoever the girl maybe but its always tricky

My punter tells me patience is the key

Then only she wouldn't be able to live without me.

You need money to please your honey.

Their is no fair play, no wrongs or rights,

Somone right down his name and also

What are the rules of the game.

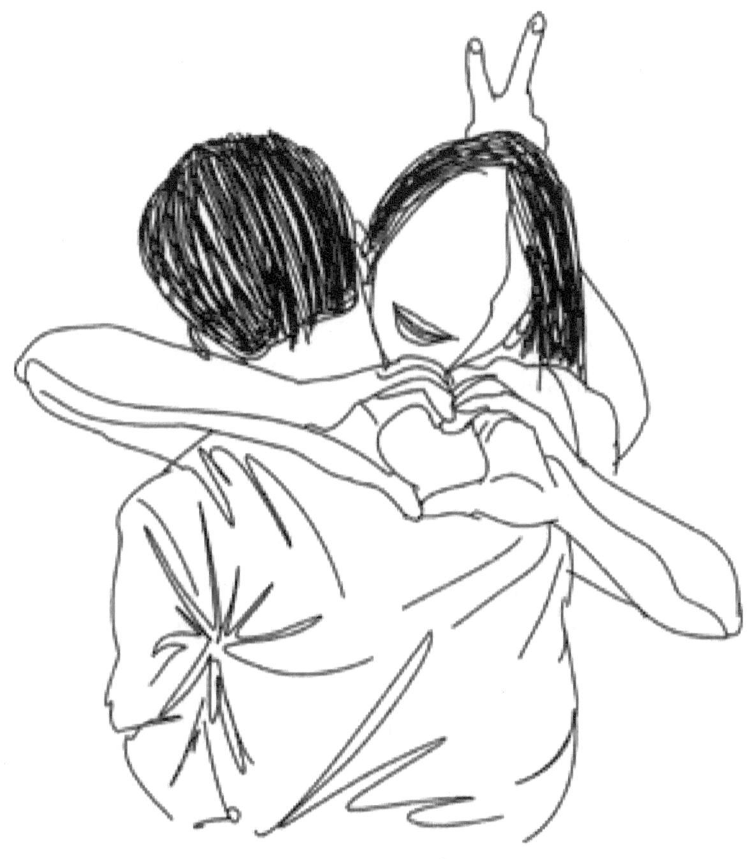

Poem 29
Change of Guard

It used to be gentle,

The times have now changed.

Lies, deceit, fakeness, fame,

Somewhere we are enraged.

Our love for truth is gone,

Every lies is a truth worth a frown.

When I munch on that burger from the deli,

I wonder are they feeding me or earning money daily.

When I walk, the speeding car wants to run me over,

Sit at home and the neighbours worry my bank balance.

Careless conversations are gone, the humming travellers are dead.

Its a photograph every step of the journey,

We fear for our life, we are mislead.

In a world of anger, hatred, and tensions,

I will open the doors of my heart and let you wish your fake intentions.

For when times will again change, I will ensure humanity survives the change of guard.

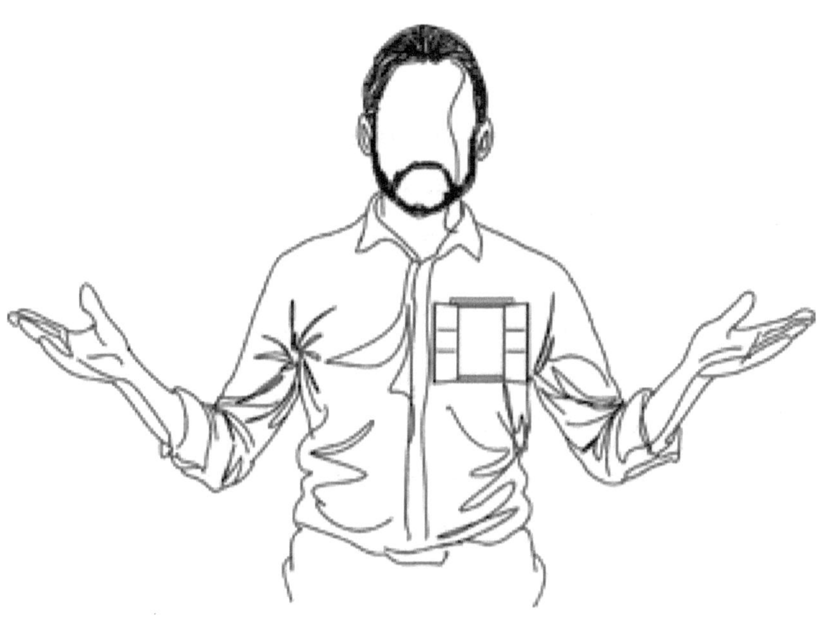

Poem 30
Anxious Breaths

Some reek of smell, some of hunger,

Some risk of alcohol, some of slumber.

But these days, everyone reeks of anxious breaths.

The hurry to prove supremacy, the hurry to prove superiority,

Dorthy richer than me, Richer than him

Study to ace the race,

Jobs have gone without a trace.

Love is a give and take not what you make,

People dying an anxious death.

For where is the peace, where are the flakes,

We are breathing heavily, snow is naked, and real as fake.

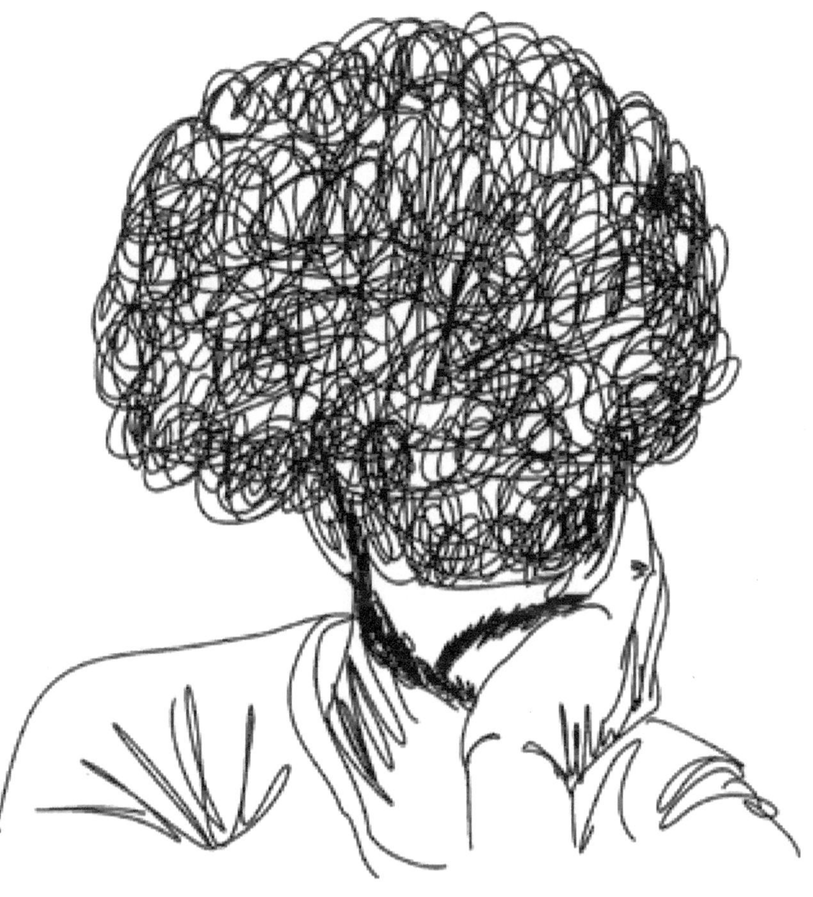

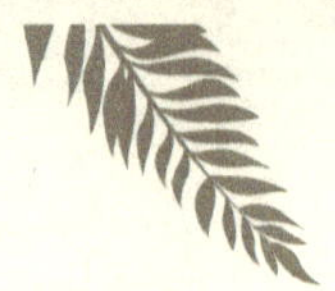

The Future - Children

Hope and tomorrow are synonymous with children who are the future of everything. We rob their smiles with the ever-changing and more upgraded greed with which we wake up every morning.

To have more, to buy more, to shop more, to build more and more concrete. The children have something to say about it!

Poem 31
The Child with a Dry Smile

Worrying, looking at the world with silent eyes

She saw the bloodshed, the bombs, the missiles.

The glaciers melted into her tears,

They cared so less about the children who grew slowly in the regions of Asia.

The economies raged, the rich wanted more,

The more they wanted, the less the children played

Parks were gone, park benches became shops,

And while they were building their greed, innocence went for a walk,

Now the children nod and play and smile a dry smile. .

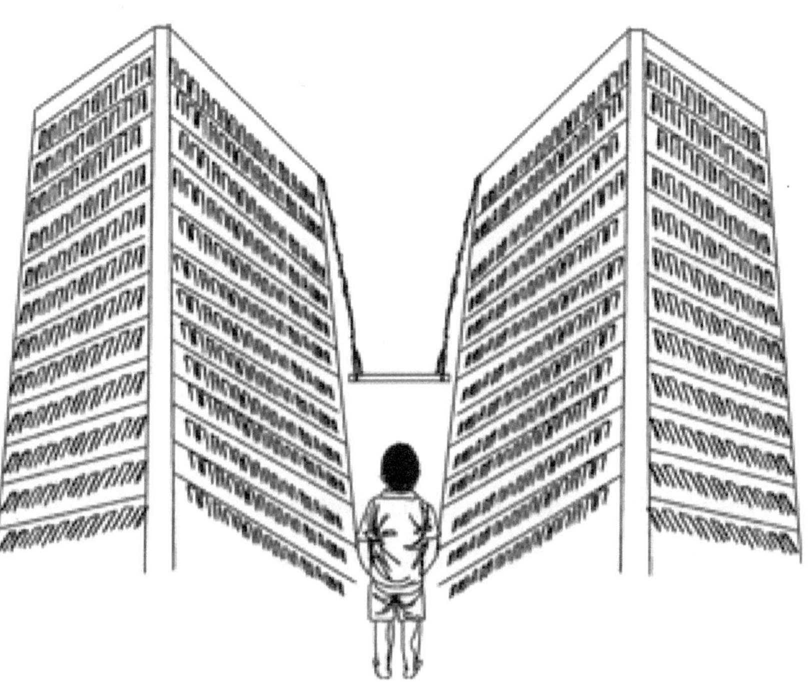

Poem 32
The World in Her Eyes

With tiny beautiful eyes,
She looks a bit mesmerized.

With dances and hearty laughs around her,
She is smiling, crying and an observing wanderer.

In a world that is amiss of love and happiness,
My little daughter is a bundle of cuteness.

Numbers, alphabets and toys are her universe,
I now have another way of looking at the world.
Through her eyes, through her eyes.

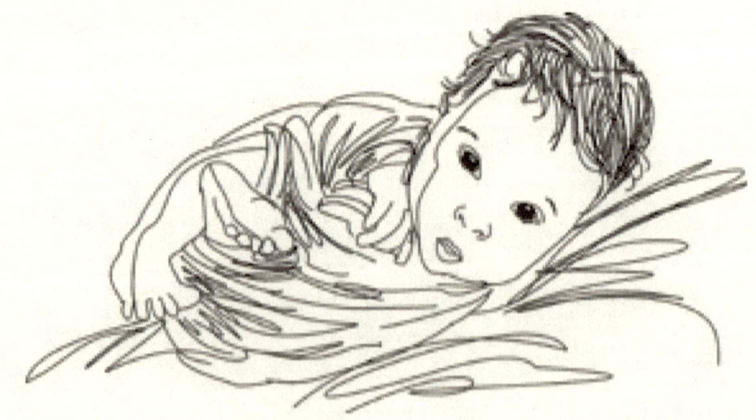

Poem 33
The Still Pool Water

Chlorine provides the blue in it,
An artificial rodent synthetic blue.

The rich swim with their awkward bodies,
Polluting the pool with money and their urine.

I sing praises of resorts and hotels,
Hiding my love handles and fatty thighs.

The still pool water absorbs it, All silently and vehemently.
The richness, dryness of souls and humans.

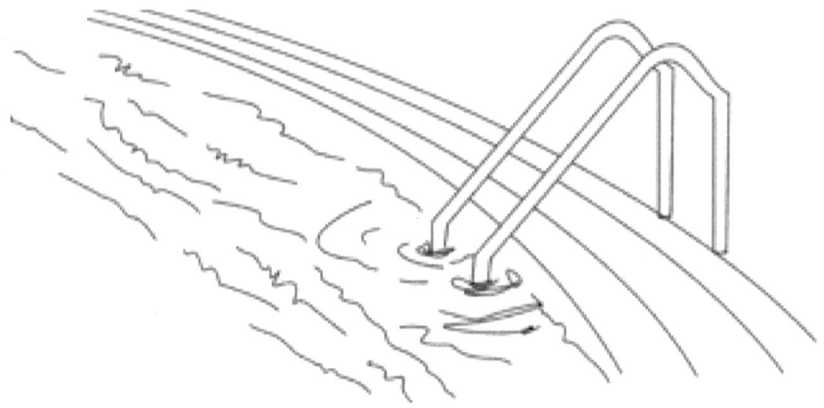

Poem 34
Arrogant Ocean Blue

The waves come and touch me,
Sometimes with force, sometimes filling me with water.

New couples hold each other in fear,
Old couples hang on to them don't die before me dear.

Do the waves have a heart,
I sit and wonder.

As they frown and thunder.

The oceans are arrogant news,
There was water, now it is gone.

The waves wipe out each one of us,
Some plant trees to stop the mayhem.
Its blue, still is, but now,
It's an arrogant ocean blue.

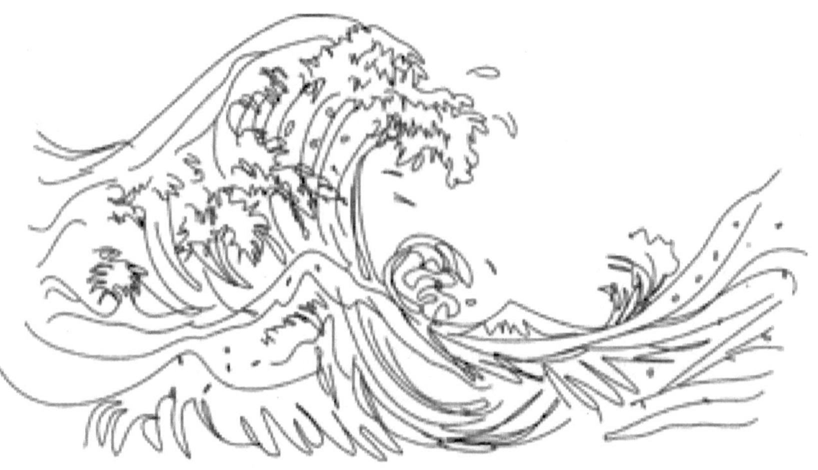

Poem 35
Thankless Us

We board the planes, never thanking the clouds.

We push and shove in queues, never thanking the crowds.

We add more people to mother earth, never thanking the ground beneath us.

We walk in and out of doors, never thanking the door-keepers.

We hog and wine and dine, never thanking the servers.

Where are we running, how thankless we have become.

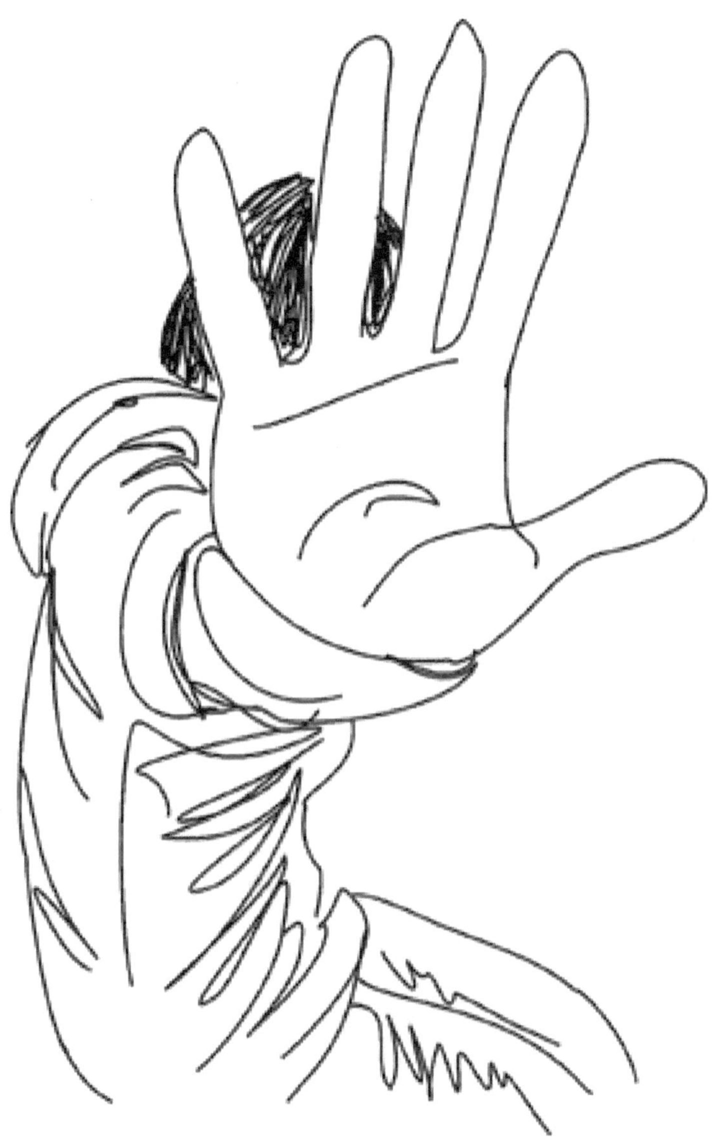

Poem 36
Lessons Can't be Learnt

We used to respect them, now we pay them to teach.

Where the young head bowed in fear and respect,
The wealthy and informed parent now bugs decisions.

Where morals were taught,
Correcting teens is often an after thought.

Where basic virtues were taught,
Now more money is sought.

Where we used to call those who taught teachers,
They have been replaced by godmen and preachers.

Where they used to carry crayons and what not,
It's sarcasm, disrespect, guns and what not.

We will learn that lessons can't be learnt.

We need those who teach and nurture, 'cos then only lessons can be learnt.

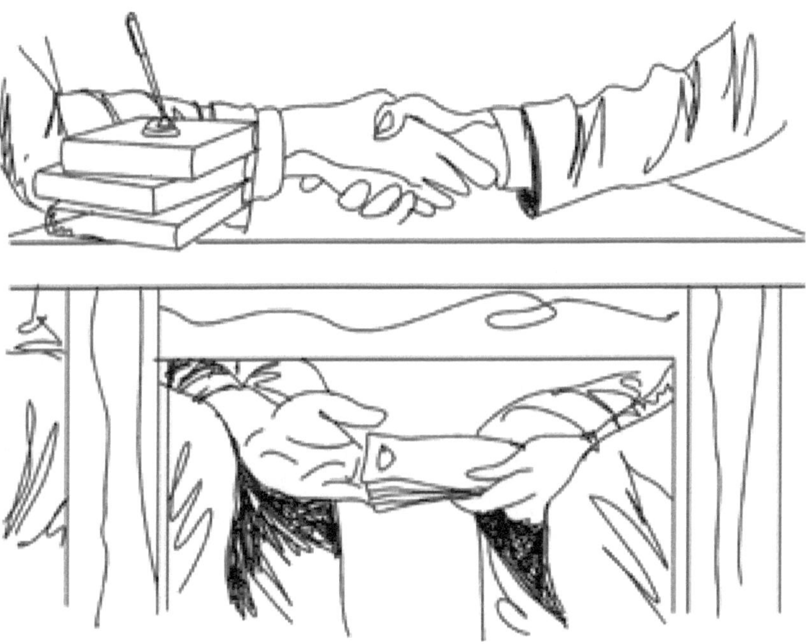

Poem 37
Before You Go

If the flies and doves,

The moments and wasps come flying talking to you.

The hair you furl, the lips you curl.

Don't trust your head,

Feign you are sad and walk away leaving blue.

'Cos when you are seen in a distant green.

I wallup(Prepare) the horses and gallop across the fields.

If you're going to be gone ,

Catch the train before I reach.

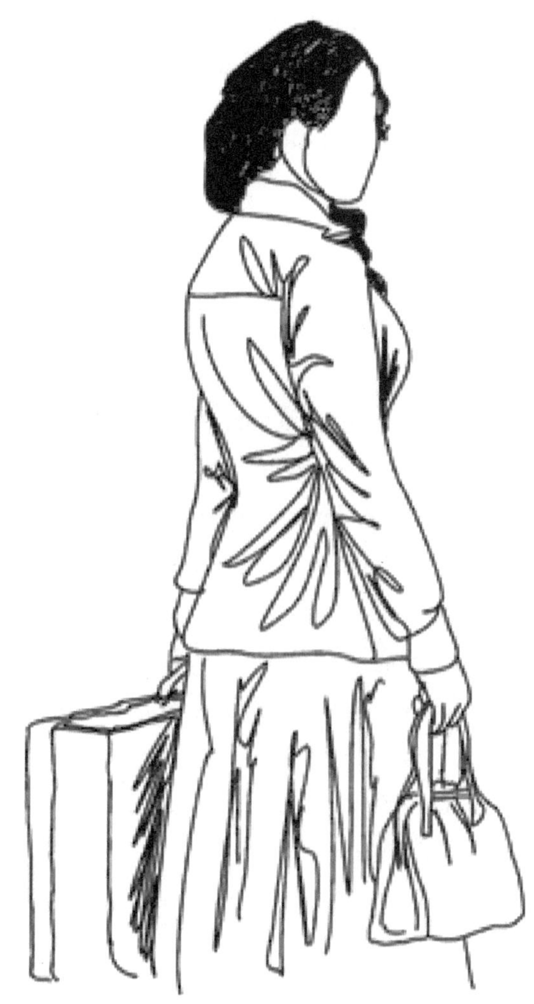

Poem 38
Concentric Circles - Dream Inside a Dream

Just got up - Where am I?

How did this happen?

I was yearning for an appearance of love,

Anxious to be hinted of affection.

An orchid of pines, apples, and pineapples beckoned me,

I stepped in and walked the narrow inviting path.

First the tiny grapes, then the enticing spares,

The fountain that has a hint of a mermaid washing herself.

I walked deep into the forest.

I looked back in a moment of concern,

The path had been washed away. The forest had me.

The concrete was too hard for my sensitivity,

Couldn't go back. The forest too soft for a slap on my lonely streak.

Answers too many and dreams a plenty,

Breaking a circle of questions, I tried to sleep again.

Or let's say, I just closed my eyes.

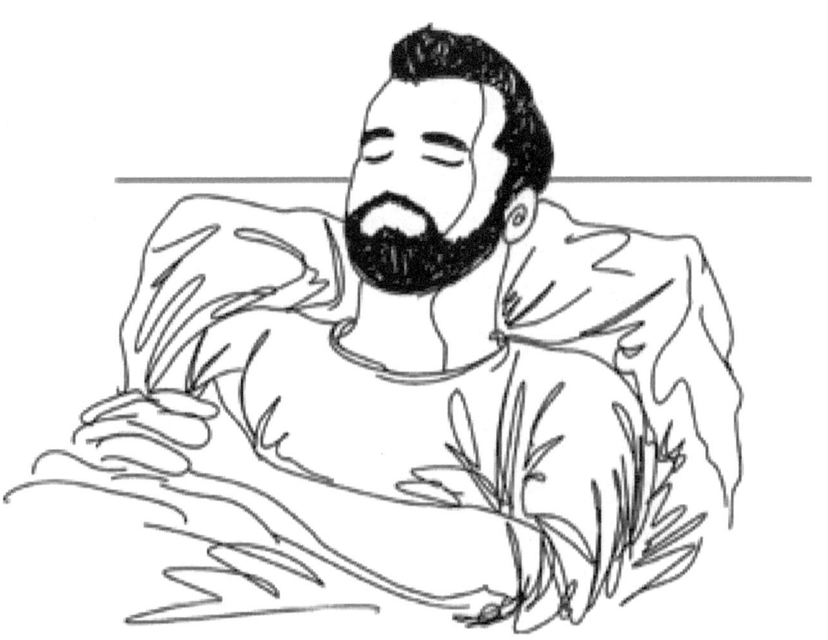

Poem 39
An Empty Paper, Sketches Itself

Wind in my hair, patterns in my head.

I stack inspiration away, near, on my desk.

Impatient to create, I think and collect ideas.

While hanging to the rails in a train.

Sipping warm-caffeine in the morning rush,

Walking, dreaming.

I surf, research, and draw.

I draw and create on my desk,

Collect ideas like crayons when away.

My ideas are determined, not to forget, not to sway.

Like a painting that sketches itself on an empty piece of paper.

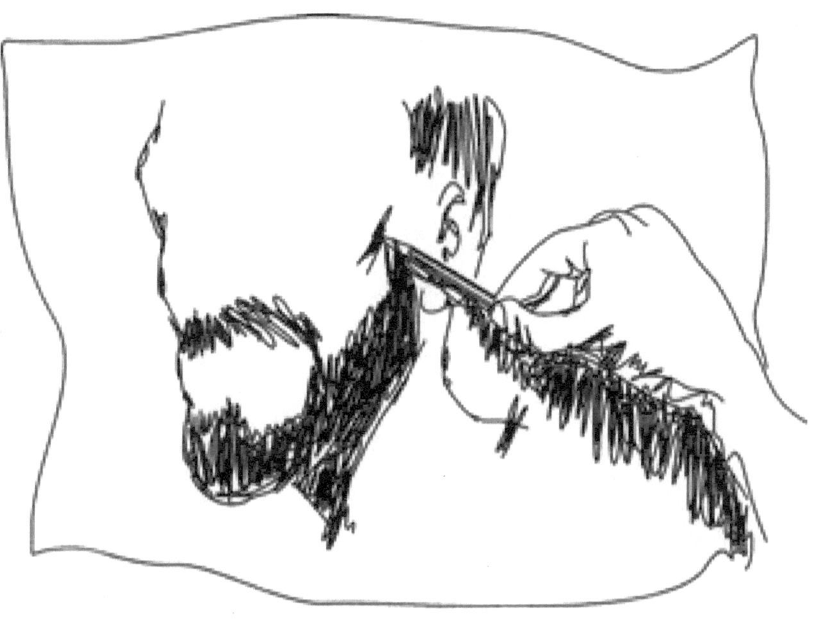

www.ingramcontent.com/pod-product-compliance
Lightning Source LLC
LaVergne TN
LVHW091727190726
843493LV00001B/478